Hello! I am a llama.

Llamas are "domesticated" and not found in the wild.

A domesticated animal lives with people, gets taken care of, and becomes part of the family.

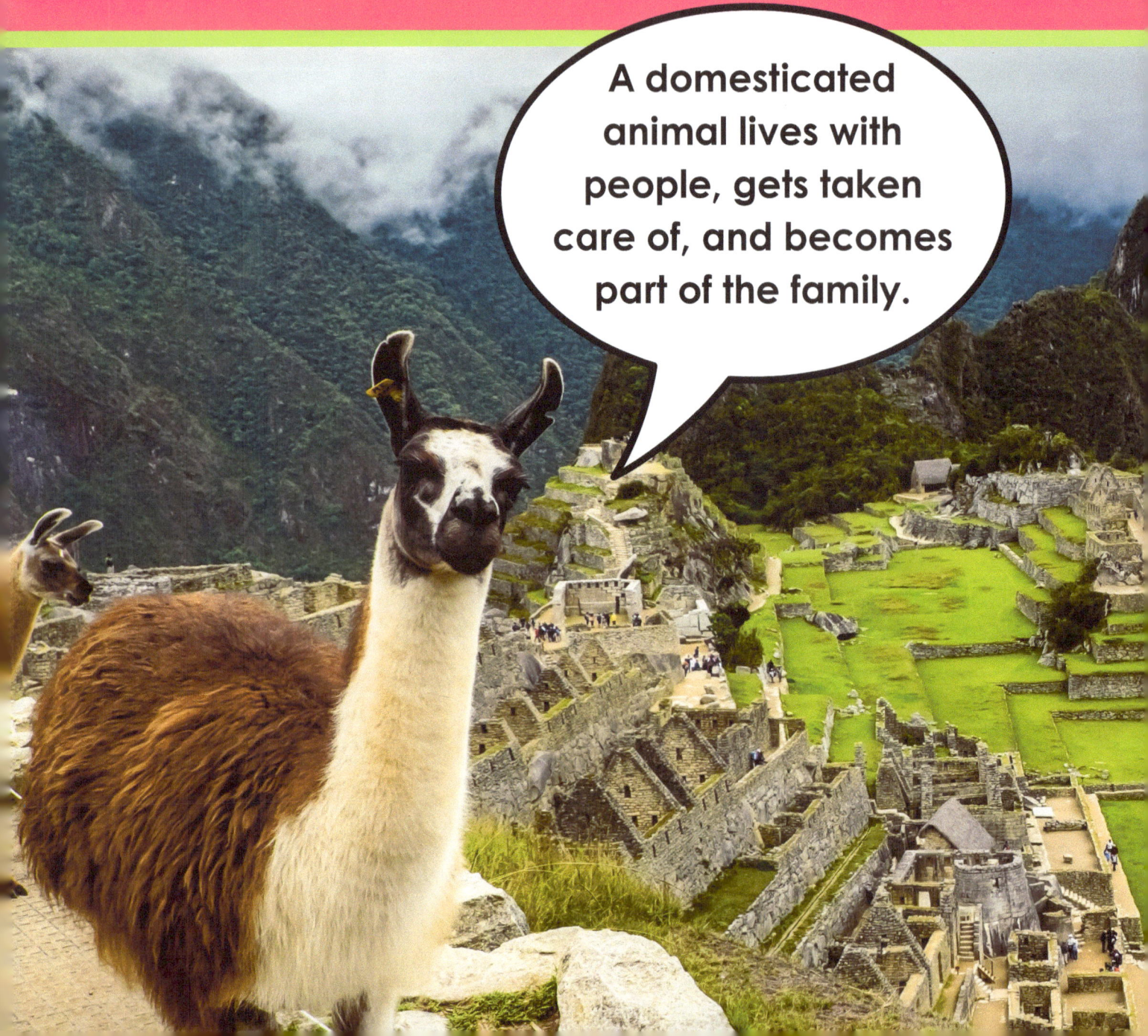

Llamas originally come from South America.

Even though llamas are big, they are not heavy.

I use my speedy legs for fun or to run away from things that scare me.

Llamas can run as fast as 35 miles per hour!

Llamas have big eyes that help them see well during the day.

Llamas can turn their ears in different directions.

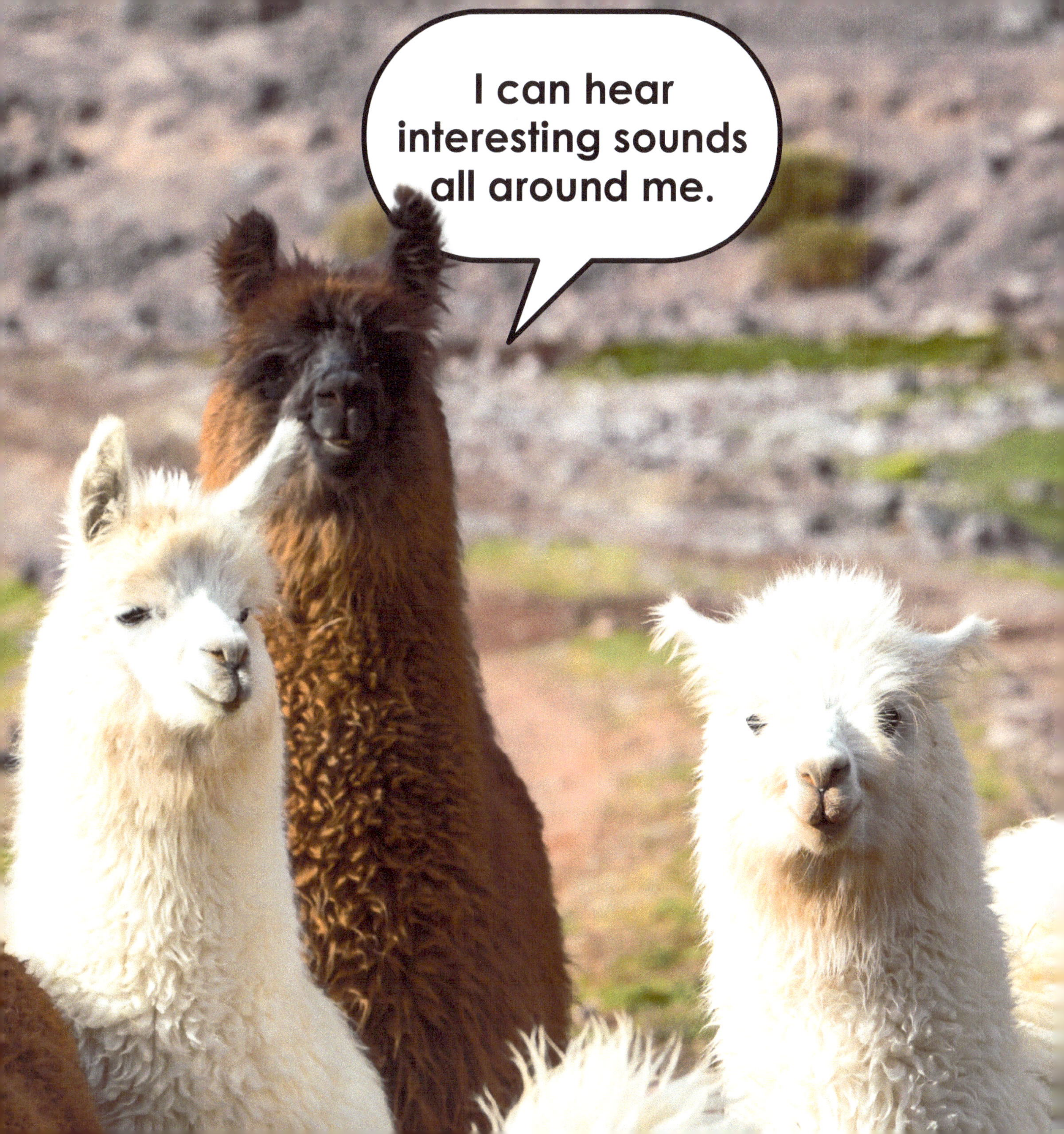
I can hear interesting sounds all around me.

Smelling is one way llamas communicate.

Smelling helps me detect changes happening around me.

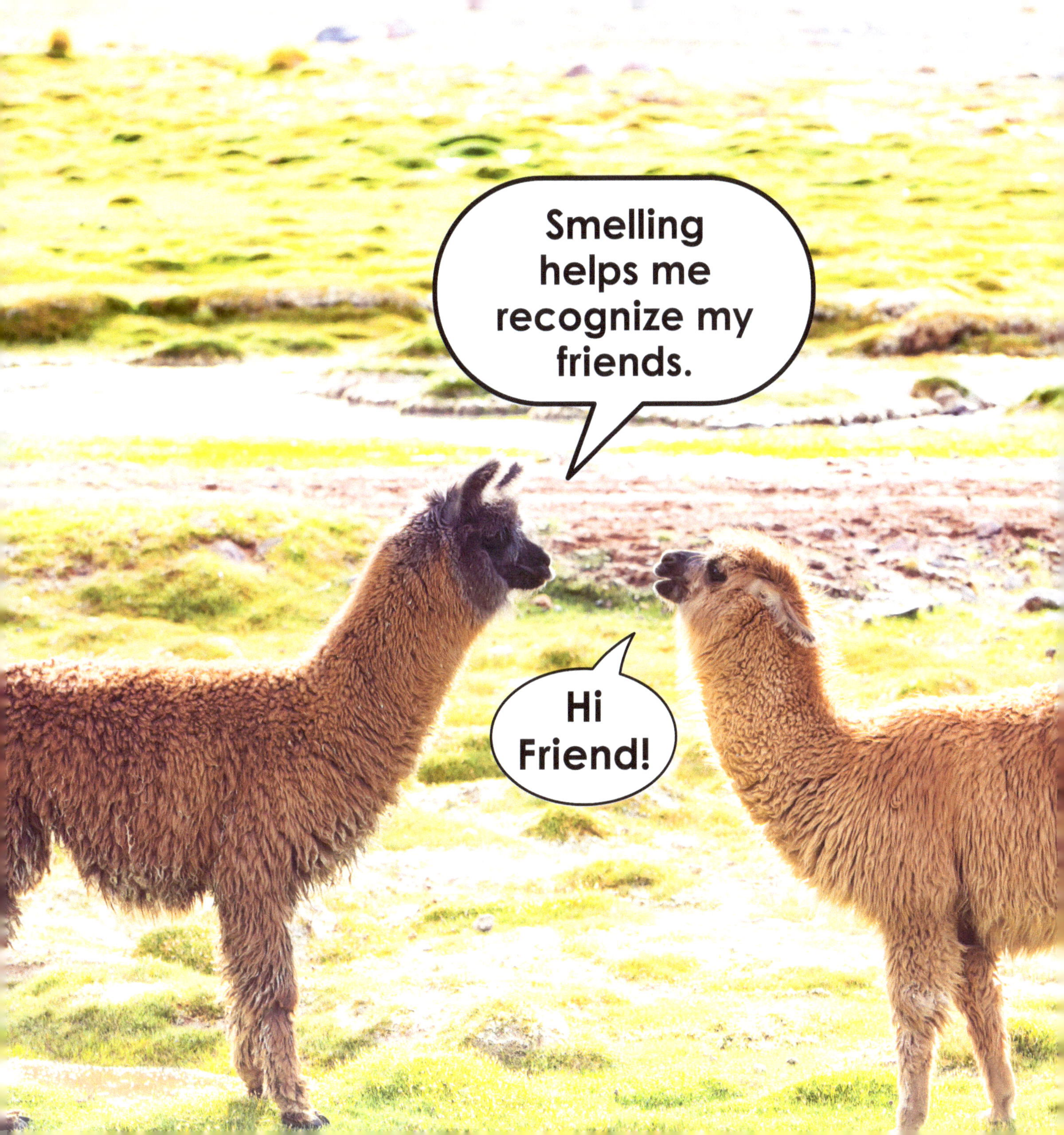
Smelling helps me recognize my friends.
Hi Friend!

Llamas stand about 4 feet (1.2m) tall at their shoulders.

Are you taller than a llama?

A llama's thick fur keeps them warm. It can look and feel different for every llama.

Llamas are "herbivores", that means they eat plants.

It's important that I eat a balanced diet to stay healthy and happy.

Llamas enjoy munching on grass and hay.

I also love a tasty treat of carrots!

Llamas often sleep while standing too.

Living in a group helps llamas stay safe.

We live in groups called "herds".

Llamas are social creatures.

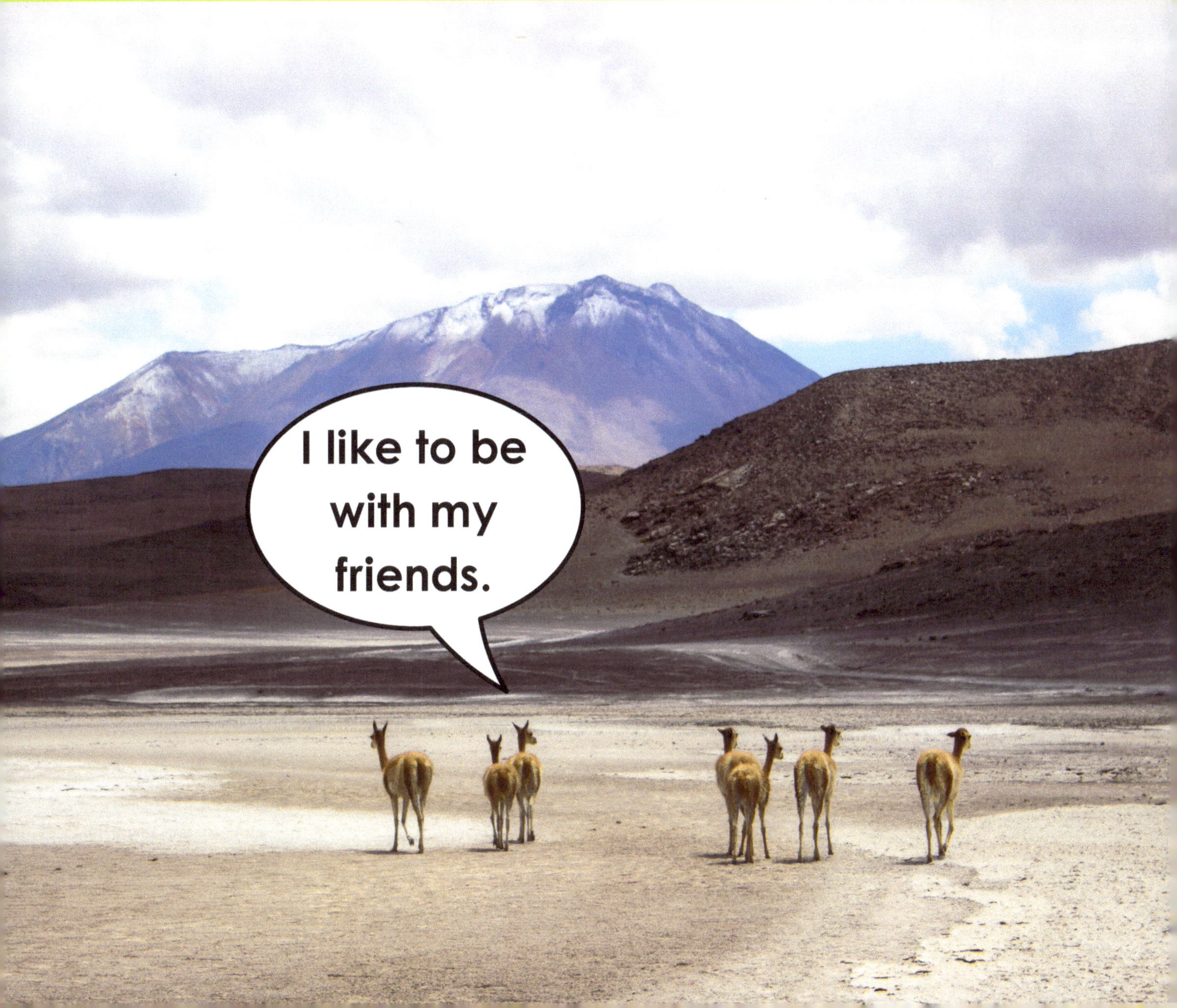

Llamas are affectionate animals.

You're my friend!

I like to nuzzle or hum to show I like you.

Llamas communicate by humming, making soft clucking sounds, or even spitting!

Nobody likes it when I spit.

Spitting can show that they are unhappy or uncomfortable.

Llamas are known for their unique and loving personalities.

Llamas are social, smart, and protective.

Older llamas usually take care
of the younger ones.

Baby llamas are called "crias".

We are going to stay close together so I can protect and love you.

It is fun to be with my llama herd!

Llamas groom each other, share resting spaces, and play together to become good friends.

LLamas can walk long distances while carrying heavy things on their back.

I can walk for a long time and I am good at helping humans.

Unlike some animals, llamas don't migrate long distances.

I'll stay right here with you.

They prefer staying close to their human friends.

In South America, people celebrate special days with llamas.

Time to PARTY!

People in the Andes Mountains have been friends with llamas for over 4,000 years!

Llamas can live for a long time, usually between 15 to 25 years.

That is longer than most pets.

Hello parents!

scan here

Visit us to find out about new releases and *FREE* offers. We'll let you know when we have a new release coming out and how you can get it for FREE.

And you can cast your vote for what book we make next!

ActiveBrainsBooks.com

or visit here

scan here

Let us know what you think. As an independent publisher, your honest reviews mean a lot to us and our business. We'd love to hear from you!

amazon.com/review/create-review/

or visit here

FOLLOW US on Amazon.

amazon.com/author/activebrainsbooks

ActiveBrainsBooks.com

ACTIVE BRAINS

www.ingramcontent.com/pod-product-compliance
Lightning Source LLC
Chambersburg PA
CBHW060844270326
41933CB00003B/190